barbecue

and marinades

Notes

1. Standard level spoon measurements are used in all recipes.
1 tablespoon = one 15 ml spoon
1 teaspoon = one 5 ml spoon

2. Both imperial and metric measurements have been given in all recipes. Use one set of measurements only and not a mixture of both.

3. Eggs should be medium unless otherwise stated. The Department of Health advises that eggs should not be consumed raw. This book contains dishes made with raw or lightly cooked eggs. It is prudent for more vulnerable people such as pregnant and nursing mothers, invalids, the elderly, babies and young children to avoid uncooked or lightly cooked dishes made with eggs. Once prepared, these dishes should be kept refrigerated and used promptly.

4. Milk should be full fat unless otherwise stated.

5. Fresh herbs should be used unless otherwise stated. If unavailable, use dried herbs as an alternative but halve the quantities stated.

6. Pepper should be freshly ground black pepper unless otherwise stated.

7. Nuts and nut derivatives
This book includes dishes made with nuts and nut derivatives. It is advisable for customers with known allergic reactions to nuts and nut derivatives and those who may be potentially vulnerable to these allergies, such as pregnant and nursing mothers, invalids, the elderly, babies and children, to avoid dishes made with nuts and nut oils. It is also prudent to check the labels of pre-prepared ingredients for the possible inclusion of nut derivatives.

8. Vegetarians should look for the 'V' symbol on a cheese to ensure it is made with vegetarian rennet. There are vegetarian forms of Parmesan, Feta, Cheddar, Cheshire, Red Leicester, dolcelatte and many goats' cheeses, among others.

barbecue

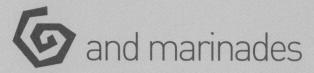 and marinades

text Sylvie Tardrew

photographs Marcel Duffas

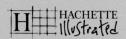 HACHETTE Illustrated

preface

Summertime means time spent in the garden, on the patio, out in the open air. The barbecue and the griddle are the order of the day. It's the season to invite friends round, to celebrate, to have the company of your guests around you as you go about preparing the food. The season of informality: no tables to lay, no entrance to make, no dressing up – just a comfortable sense of well-being. Remember to provide lots of chairs and double up on the usual amount of cutlery, plates and glasses. Everybody will be on the move – mingling, chatting, going from table to table, strolling beneath the trees. Barbecuing is hot and thirsty work, so be sure you have plenty of refreshing drinks available – and don't forget the ice. The expert barbecue organiser knows how to make life simple and will have prepared the sauces and marinades the day before and lit the barbecue several hours ahead of time, ready for use the moment the first guests arrive. The smart apron he or she will, of course, be wearing serves the dual purpose of protecting the clothes and making sure the role as chef is recognised by everyone!

Sylvie Tardrew

 marinades

Aromatic olive oil

Makes 1 litre
(1³/₄ pints)

**250 ml (8 fl oz)
lemon juice**

**2 small pieces
Espelette pepper**

**750 ml (1¼ pints)
olive oil**

**3 cayenne peppers
or small chillies**

**1 stalk fresh lemon
grass**

1 star anise

**1 garlic clove,
peeled**

1. Put all the ingredients into a clean bottle and close firmly.

2. Shake well and let stand in the refrigerator for 1–2 days before using.

*(Suggestion: Espelette pepper from the Basque country should be available from specialist shops.
If not, use 1 small piece of dried chilli.)*

TIP

THIS OIL can be kept for 30 days.

Aromatic wine vinegar

Makes 1 litre
(1³/₄ pints)

1 clove

1 spring onion

**1 litre (1³/₄ pints)
good quality wine
vinegar**

2 bay leaves

1 sprig rosemary

**2 garlic cloves,
unpeeled**

1. Stick the clove into the onion. Put all the ingredients into a clean bottle and close firmly.

2. Stand for 48 hours in the refrigerator before using.

TIP

THIS VINEGAR can be used to sprinkle on grilled red meats and fish when they are cooked.

Coconut milk marinade

Makes about 750 ml
(1¼ pints)

2 cans coconut milk

**8 tablespoons
lemon juice**

**1 teaspoon curry
powder**

1 pinch saffron

**1 tablespoon dried
parsley**

rind of 1 lemon

rind of 1 lime

**small pinch cayenne
pepper**

**2 tablespoons
groundnut or
sunflower oil**

1. Mix all the ingredients together.

2. If the marinade seems too thick,
add a little milk.

TASTE BITE
THE FLAVOURS in this
marinade will enhance all
kinds of fish.

Spiced marinade

Quantity for 1 kg
(2 lb) meat

4 tablespoons white wine

2 tablespoons wine vinegar

2 sprigs tarragon

1 West Indian pepper (or 1 very hot chilli), finely chopped

2 spring onions, finely chopped

1 teaspoon black pepper

1 tablespoon grated fresh ginger (or 1 teaspoon ground ginger)

1 teaspoon ground allspice

1 teaspoon dried thyme

1. Mix all the ingredients in a bowl.

2. Add the meat to the marinade and stir to coat well. Set aside for no longer than 1 hour as this mixture is very hot.

3. Before putting the meat (beef or pork) on the grill, drain and pat dry with kitchen paper. Season with salt once it is cooked.

TIP

TIME PERMITTING, the beef or pork should be brought to room temperature before marinating to allow the flavours to permeate the meat.

Japanese marinade

Quantity for 1 kg
(2 lb) fish

**4 tablespoons soy
sauce**

**4 tablespoons
sesame oil**

**4 tablespoons rice
wine**

1 tablespoon sugar

**2 spring onions
(including stem),
finely chopped**

**2 garlic cloves,
crushed**

**1 teaspoon chopped
fresh ginger**

1. Mix the ingredients together in a
bowl and cover with clingfilm.

2. Stand the marinade in the
refrigerator for at least 30 minutes
before using.

TIP
ALWAYS TASTE any
grilled fish before adding
seasoning.

Dry marinade

Quantity for 1 kg
(2 lb) meat

**2 tablespoons
paprika**

**1 tablespoon
ground cumin**

**1 tablespoon
chopped thyme**

**1 onion, finely
chopped**

**2 garlic cloves,
crushed**

**1 tablespoon dried
oregano**

**6 peppercorns,
crushed**

**1 bay leaf, in 3–4
pieces**

**1 teaspoon cayenne
pepper**

1 teaspoon olive oil

1. Put all the ingredients except the oil into a mortar.

2. Mix and pound thoroughly with the pestle.

3. Add the olive oil to make a smooth marinade before spreading it on the meat.

TASTE BITE
THERE ARE NO LIMITS to the changes one can ring with dry marinades. Try adding other spices like cardamom, cinnamon, pink peppercorns, coriander, star anise, curry powder…

large dishes

Haddock with aromatic herbs

Serves 6

3 large slices fresh haddock

3 cinnamon sticks (or 1 teaspoon ground cinnamon)

1 stick fresh lemon grass

4 sprigs lemon thyme

1 teaspoon coriander seeds

1 teaspoon pink peppercorns

5 peppercorns

2 bay leaves

1 shallot, halved

2 garlic cloves

juice of 2–3 limes

7 tablespoons olive oil

salt, pepper

1. Mix the marinade ingredients in a deep dish, season with salt and pepper. Put the fish in the marinade and set aside for 2 hours, turning the pieces at least once.

2. Bring the barbecue to a fairly high temperature, brush the fish with oil and lay on the barbecue to sear. Cook for 3–4 minutes on either side.

3. Remove the centre bone from the fish and divide into portions.

TASTE BITE
THIS EXCELLENT FISH would go well with a tomato salad, a salad of French beans, or with baked potatoes.

Rib of beef, or 'chuleta'

Serves 6

2 thick beef ribs, about 600 g (1¼ lb) each

1 tablespoon olive oil

2 bay leaves

few sprigs thyme

Aromatic Wine Vinegar (see page 10)

salt, pepper

1. Take the beef out of the refrigerator and allow it to come to room temperature before cooking.

2. Rub the oil into the meat, then press the bay leaves, broken into small pieces, and the leaves rubbed from the thyme all over the surface of the meat.

3. Sear the ribs on the very hot barbecue for 5 minutes to form a crust, then turn them over and repeat the process on the other side.

4. Lift the grill on the barbecue and cook for a further 10 minutes on each side.

5. Remove the meat from the barbecue and immediately sprinkle with the Aromatic Wine Vinegar. Season with salt and pepper, carve and serve.

 TIP

IF THE BONE IS REMOVED before cooking, it will be easier to carve the meat into neat slices for serving.

Veal cutlets with paprika

Serves 6

6 veal cutlets

1 tablespoon paprika

1 tablespoon olive oil

4 tablespoons lemon juice

juice of whole orange

salt, pepper

1. In a dish, mix together half of the paprika, all the olive oil, the lemon and orange juice and season with salt and pepper.

2. Marinade the cutlets in this mixture for 1 hour, turning them over at least once.

3. Drain the cutlets, place them on the griddle and grill for 10 minutes on each side.

4. Dust with the rest of the paprika and serve very hot.

TASTE BITE
SERVE A SALAD of red onions with these cutlets.

Sea bream Spanish style

Serves 6

2 sea bream, gutted and scaled

20 garlic cloves, peeled

3 tablespoons olive oil

1 dried Espelette pepper, or dried chilli

sherry vinegar

salt, pepper

1. Remove the skin from the garlic then slice finely. Finely chop the pepper.

2. Brush 1 tablespoon of the oil over the fish and stuff them with the garlic and dried Espelette pepper, or dried chilli.

3. Clamp them into special fish baskets and cook over the hot embers for 10–15 minutes either side.

4. Remove the fish from the baskets and lay on a serving dish. Open them out carefully and remove the bones, then season the fish with salt and pepper and drizzle over the remaining 2 tablespoons of olive oil. Sprinkle with a few drops of sherry vinegar and serve immediately.

 TIP

THE FISH-SHAPED WIRE BASKETS used in this recipe allow one to handle and turn fish easily, without damaging them. They are particularly recommended for sea bream and bass.

Swordfish Mexican style

Serves 6

2 large slices swordfish

4 garlic cloves, crushed

1 tablespoon green pepper paste

1 tablespoon paprika

1 sprig dried oregano

3 tablespoons rum or tequila (optional)

7 tablespoons canned pineapple juice

coriander

1 red onion, finely chopped

salt, pepper

1. Mix all the ingredients, except the fish, in a deep dish, season with salt and pepper.

2. Lay the swordfish in this marinade and let stand for 2 hours, turning the slices over once.

3. Heat the griddle or barbecue then drain the swordfish slices and grill them for 5–8 minutes on each side over medium heat.

4. Correct the seasoning if necessary and serve very hot.

 TASTE BITE

PLANTAINS would go well with this dish.

Salmon steaks with bacon

Serves 6

6 salmon steaks, about 150 g (5 oz) each

1 tablespoon olive oil

12 slices bacon

sea salt, pepper

1. Heat the barbecue and brush oil over the fish.

2. When the barbecue is very hot, place the salmon steaks onto it, skin side down, and cook until they turn pinkish (they should be almost raw in the centre).

3. At the last moment, rapidly grill the bacon slices and lay two on each piece of fish. Season with salt and pepper and serve immediately.

TASTE BITE

BAKED POTATOES would go perfectly with this dish. Don't forget to serve crème fraîche and salted butter with them.

Fillets of red mullet with fennel

Serves 6

18 fillets red mullet, scaled

3–4 fennel sticks (or dill)

1 tablespoon olive oil

salt, pepper

1. Break up the fennel sticks and crumble them to shreds.

2. Brush both sides of the fillets with oil and lay them on a dish. Scatter over the shreds of fennel and set aside for 20 minutes to allow the flavour of the fennel to mingle with the fish.

3. Bring the barbecue up to a fierce heat and sear the mullet fillets very quickly on each side. Season with salt and pepper.

TASTE BITE

SERVE THESE FILLETS warm on a salad of mange-tout dressed with lemon juice.

Leg of lamb shepherd style

Serves 8

**leg of lamb
weighing 2.5 kg
(5 lb)**

**2 tablespoons olive
oil**

**2 tablespoons
rosemary**

3 sprigs thyme

3 bay leaves

**1 garlic clove,
crushed**

salt, pepper

1. Light the barbecue well in advance: a lot of very hot embers will be required to produce the necessary heat.

2. Rub the meat with the oil and strew the rosemary, thyme, bay leaves and garlic all over it. Season with salt and pepper.

3. Lay 7 large sheets of aluminium foil in a stack and place the leg of lamb in the centre. Cover with 7 more sheets and fold in the edges to make a large, sealed parcel. Lay it on the grill of the barbecue.

4. Leave to cook for 15 minutes on each side then repeat the process for 10 more minutes on each side.

5. Leave it to rest, either on the grill lifted to the highest level, or on the side of the barbecue, until you are ready to eat.

 TIP

PREPARED IN THIS way, the leg of lamb will not have a crisp skin, but will be very tender and full of flavour. In addition, it can safely be left to await late-comers; it will stay hot and be perfectly cooked.

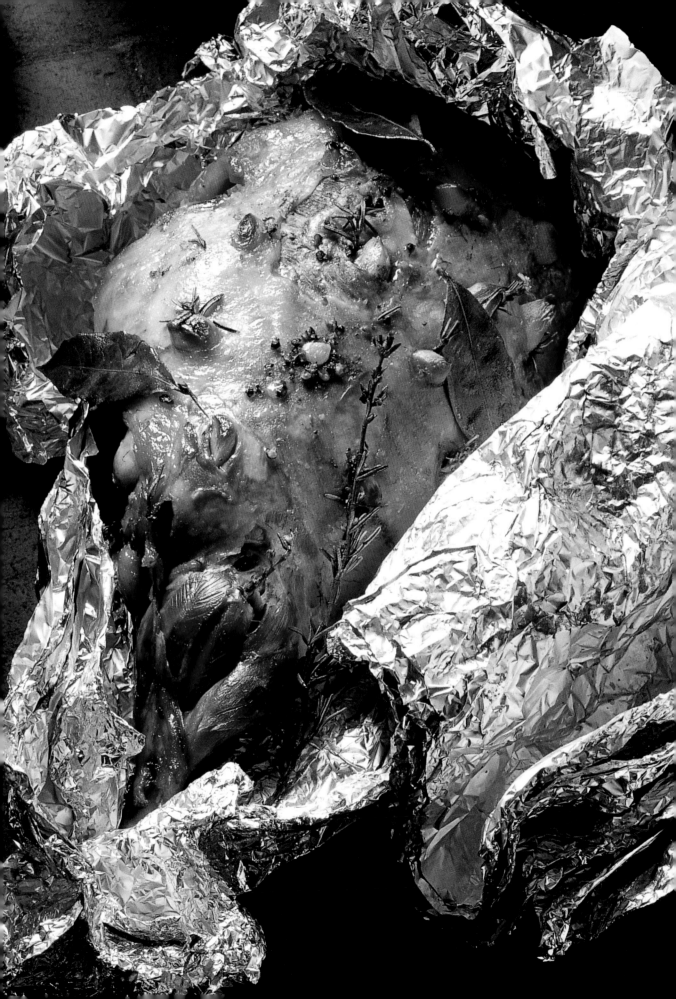

Bread

Makes 3 flat,
round loaves

**300 ml ('/₂ pint)
warm water**

**1 sachet baker's
yeast**

**500 g (1 lb) strong
white plain flour**

**2 tablespoons olive
oil**

1 teaspoon salt

1. Mix the yeast with the warm water. When it begins to foam, pour it on the flour, then add half the olive oil and all the salt.

2. Knead the dough until it becomes supple to the touch. Place it in a large bowl, cover with a damp cloth and leave for 2 hours at room temperature.

3. When the dough is well risen, knead it again for a few minutes, divide it into 3 and roll into balls, then flatten them to form round loaves.

4. Cook them on a very hot griddle, previously brushed with the rest of the oil. When the dough puffs up, turn the bread over and cook for a further few minutes.

TASTE BITE

YOU CAN VARY THIS THEME by sprinkling the dough with sesame or poppy seeds, or even rubbed thyme, before cooking.

Chicken in a cornmeal coating

Serves 6

**12 chicken
drumsticks**

**200 g (7 oz)
cornmeal**

**2 tablespoons
corn oil**

salt, pepper

◎ TASTE BITE

THIS IS A TYPICALLY
AMERICAN DISH; don't lose
the opportunity to serve
chips with it!

1. Place the barbecue grill down on the embers to get it nice and hot.

2. Put the cornmeal in a paper or a plastic bag.

3. Give the drumsticks a light coating of oil and season with salt and pepper.

4. Holding each drumstick by the end of the bone, dip it into the cornmeal in the bag then shake off the excess.

5. Cook them on the grill of the barbecue for 15 minutes either side then eat them with your fingers!

Chicken Mauritian style

Serves 6

6 chicken drumsticks (or 6 chicken breasts)

1 large onion, finely chopped

3 garlic cloves, crushed (new season garlic, if possible)

375 g (12 oz) full-fat yogurt

2–3 drops piquant sauce

1 bunch coriander, chopped

1 teaspoon ground cumin

¹/₂ teaspoon ground turmeric

1 teaspoon garam masala

8 tablespoons lemon juice

salt, pepper

1. Mix together all the marinade ingredients.

2. Add the drumsticks or chicken breasts to the marinade and let stand for half a day.

3. Lift out the pieces, without allowing them to drain too much, and lay them on the grill of a barbecue that has been lit for some time, or on a griddle.

4. Cook them for 15 minutes on either side, raising the grill if the meat is in danger of burning (or lower the heat).

TASTE BITE
SERVE THE DRUMSTICKS on a green salad, with a good, fresh herb dressing.

Marinated tuna

Serves 6

**3 slices tuna, 2 cm
($^3/_4$ inch) thick,
trimmed**

**1 tablespoon olive
oil**

1 clove

**1 carrot, peeled
and cut in rings**

**1 onion, finely
chopped**

**1 garlic clove,
crushed**

2 bay leaves

4 sprigs thyme

**sea salt,
peppercorns**

1. Make a marinade with all the
ingredients, except the tuna, in a deep
dish.

2. Lay the tuna slices in the marinade,
turning them over several times so that
they become well coated.

3. Cover with clingfilm and leave in a
cool place for 3 hours, remembering
to turn the fish again at least once.

4. Prepare the barbecue. When the
embers are glowing, remove the tuna
slices from the marinade, drain, and
dry them on kitchen paper.

5. Cook the fish quickly for barely
3 minutes on either side if you like it
'blue', or a little longer if you prefer
it less rare.

 TASTE BITE
A TOMATO COULIS with
basil served with this dish
would be a perfect com-
pliment to the flavours of
the marinade.

 TIP
BE CAREFUL WITH THE
TIMING. Even if you don't
like it 'blue' you should not
cook tuna for too long or it
will become very dry.

Barbecued T-bone steak

Serves about 8–10

1 thick T-bone steak, approx 2 kg (4 lb)

Dry Marinade (see page 16)

salt, pepper

barbecue sauce, to serve

TIP

THE T-BONE is a large cut of beef that includes part of the fillet and part of the sirloin steak. It is a great favourite with meat lovers.

1. Spread the Dry Marinade on a large plate. Lay the piece of meat on it, turning it to coat thoroughly with the mixture. Leave for at least 1 hour at room temperature, then turn it over again and leave for 1 further hour.

2. Place the barbecue grill in the lowest position and when the embers are very hot, grill the T-bone for 3–4 minutes on each side.

3. Raise the grill and continue cooking for 20–30 minutes, according to the thickness of the meat, turning it over half way through.

4. Season with salt and pepper and remove the bone. Carve into slices and serve on hot plates, accompanied by a bowl of barbecue sauce.

Caramelised pork spare-ribs

Serves 6

1.5 kg (3 lb) pork spare-ribs

2 tablespoons honey

paprika

sherry vinegar

salt, pepper

1. Separate the spare-ribs and brush them over with honey. Season with salt and pepper and lightly sprinkle with paprika.

2. Lay the ribs on the hot grill and let them cook gently for 15 minutes on each side.

3. Remove the ribs from the barbecue, adjust the seasoning if necessary and sprinkle with a few drops of sherry vinegar.

4. Serve very hot, and eat them with your fingers.

 TIP

USING SUGAR IN PLACE OF THE HONEY will give a more pronounced caramel taste and texture. A light coating of oil on the spare-ribs will help the sugar adhere.

small dishes
and kebabs

Tiger prawn kebabs with Sichuan pepper

Serves 6

18 large raw tiger
prawns

1 tablespoon olive
oil

2 teaspoons
ground Sichuan
(or Chinese) pepper

2 lemons

salt

6 skewers

1. Thread 3 prawns on each skewer.

2. Brush them lightly with olive oil and lay them on a very hot barbecue; season with Sichuan pepper.

3. When they have taken on a good red colour, turn them over and grill the other side.

4. Serve immediately, very hot, seasoned with salt and plenty of Sichuan pepper and a squeeze of lemon.

TASTE BITE
THESE DELICATE AND ORIGINAL KEBABS are ideal for nibbling with an aperitif.

TIP
THIS SIMPLE TECHNIQUE can be applied equally well to other varieties of large prawns and shrimp.

Monkfish kebabs with autumn fruits

Serves 6

about 800 g (1¹/₂ lb) monkfish, cut into cubes

2 apples, each cut into 12 pieces

4 tablespoons lemon juice

2 tablespoons olive oil

48 Italian grapes

1 pinch cayenne pepper

salt, pepper

6 skewers

1. Dip the apple pieces into the lemon juice.

2. Coat the fish pieces with oil and season with salt and pepper.

3. Thread them on metal or wooden skewers, alternating with the apple pieces and the grapes.

4. Grill the kebabs quickly over a very hot barbecue for about 3 minutes each side.

5. Before serving, dust very lightly with cayenne pepper.

TASTE BITE

FINE STRIPS OF FAT BACON added to this basic recipe will give an unexpected smoky flavour.

TIP

THIS RECIPE WORKS with any firm white fish, such as cod and haddock.

Mussel kebabs

Serves 6

1 litre (1³/₄ pints)
mussels

2 garlic cloves,
crushed

2 sprigs dill

3 tablespoons olive
oil

1 tablespoon dry
white wine

12 very thin slices
bacon

1 lemon (optional)

sea salt, pepper

6 skewers

1. Prepare a marinade with the garlic, dill, oil and white wine.

2. Cook the mussels in a sauté pan over moderate heat until they open, discarding any that remain shut. Shell the mussels and drop them into the marinade. Set aside for 20 minutes.

3. Fill the skewers, threading the bacon slices like ribbons under and over each alternate mussel.

4. Cook on the barbecue for 2 minutes. Season with pepper and a light sprinkling of salt (taking the saltiness of the bacon into account) and a squeeze of lemon if liked.

TASTE BITE
THESE UNUSUAL LITTLE
KEBABS would be delicious
eaten with Fennel and Dried
Apricots (see page 94).

Tuna and chipolata kebabs

Serves 6

800 g (1½ lb) dark tuna

5 thyme sprigs

2 bay leaves

1 tablespoon sunflower or groundnut oil

24 small chipolata sausages

sea salt, pepper

6 lemon wedges

6 skewers

1. Rub the leaves from the thyme and chop them with the bay leaf. Add the oil and stir well.

2. Cut the tuna into regular cubes, roll them in the flavoured oil and set aside.

3. Cook the chipolatas on the grill until golden brown.

4. Thread the chipolatas on the skewers, alternating with the tuna.

5. Put the kebabs back on the grill and cook for 2 minutes on each side. Season with salt and pepper and serve with lemon wedges.

TIP

THE SUBTLE COMBINATION of the hint of iodine associated with fish and the smoky flavour of pork products makes an interesting theme. Another dish based on the same principle is Salmon Steaks with Bacon (see page 29).

TASTE BITE
SMALL SPICY Italian sausages or merguez (spicy North African sausages) can be used in place of the chipolatas, if preferred.

Scallop kebabs

Serves 6

**36 scallops,
cleaned and
trimmed by the
fishmonger**

**1 tablespoon
clarified butter**

olive oil

1–2 lemons

salt, pepper

6 skewers

1. Thread the scallops on skewers and brush them over with the clarified butter.

2. Cook the kebabs on the griddle for 1 minute each side; leave to grill for a few extra seconds if you prefer them a little more cooked, but no longer. Over-cooking will make them tough.

3. Season with salt and pepper, sprinkle with olive oil and a squeeze of lemon. Serve immediately.

TASTE BITE

FOR A SAUCE to serve with this dish, blend together in a liquidiser 1 tablespoon raisins with 1 tablespoon thin, clear honey, 1 teaspoon capers, 2 tablespoons olive oil, salt and pepper.

Langoustine kebabs

Serves 6

**18 Langoustines
(Dublin Bay prawns)**

1 bunch of tarragon

**100 g (3¹/₂ oz)
lightly salted
butter**

2 lemons

salt, pepper

6 skewers

1. Wash the tarragon, squeeze the water out and chop finely. Put into a food processor with the butter and blend thoroughly, or rub through a sieve.

2. Melt half of this tarragon butter in a small pan over a low heat.

3. Thread the langoustines on skewers, brush them all over with the melted tarragon butter and cook on the griddle for 5 minutes.

4. Season the kebabs with salt and pepper, garnish with lemon wedges and serve, passing round the rest of the tarragon butter separately.

TASTE BITE
PREPARE DOUBLE THE QUANTITY of tarragon butter and serve as an accompaniment to brochettes or spread on slices of crusty bread.

Sardines stuffed with herbs

Serves 6

36 sardines

2 tablespoons olive oil

1 bunch of parsley

1 bunch of basil

1 garlic clove

1 shallot

sea salt, pepper

1. Ask your fishmonger to fillet the sardines.

2. Brush oil over the skin side of each fillet.

3. Put the leaves of the parsley and basil into a food processor and process finely, together with the peeled garlic and shallot.

4. Sprinkle this herb mixture over half of the sardine fillets and cover these with the remaining ones, then line them up on a double grill.

5. Clamp the grill closed and set it over the hot coals. Cook for 2 minutes then turn the grill over and continue cooking for a further 2 minutes.

6. Open the grill and slide the sardines onto plates. Season with salt and pepper and serve.

TASTE BITE

FOR A REAL TREAT, serve a little fresh tomato salad with this dish.

TIP

THIS RECIPE is equally delicious simply baked in the oven.

Grilled sardines and anchovies

Serves 6

24 sardines

24 fresh anchovies

2 tablespoons olive oil

Aromatic Wine Vinegar (see page 10)

ground Espelette pepper or pinch of cayenne pepper

sea salt

6 skewers

1. Get the fishmonger to gut the sardines and anchovies.

2. Thread the fish, four at a time, on pre-soaked thin wooden skewers, brush them with oil and lay them on a very hot griddle.

3. Cook for 1 minute on each side.

4. Sprinkle them with Aromatic Wine Vinegar, dust with the Espelette pepper, season with salt and serve immediately.

TASTE BITE
ALL KINDS OF SMALL FISH, such as mullet, or young mackerel, are ideal for preparing in this way.

Grilled squid

Serves 6

18 small squid

2 tablespoons olive oil

ground Espelette pepper, or cayenne pepper

Aromatic Wine Vinegar (see page 10)

salt, pepper

1. Ask the fishmonger to clean the squid.

2. Wash the squid and coat quickly in the olive oil then brown on the griddle for a few minutes each side.

3. When the squid are cooked, dust with the Espelette pepper and season with salt and pepper. Just before removing them from the griddle, sprinkle the squid with Aromatic Wine Vinegar then serve.

☼ TIP

IF YOU HAVE HAD TO SETTLE FOR LARGER SQUID they will need pre-cooking for a while in boiling water or their texture may be rubbery.

Mussels cooked on pine needles

Serves 6

9 litres (8 quarts) mussels

2 armfuls of pine needles

 TIP

WARNING: This procedure is spectacular but dangerous and should never be used in a forest, a pine wood, or anywhere else where fire could quickly take hold.

1. Scrape the mussels carefully, removing the beards, and rinse several times under running water.

2. Closely pack them side by side on the grill, hinge side down.

3. Prepare the barbecue with a thick layer of pine needles and set light to them, taking care to stand well back. Place the grill with the mussels on the needles and cover it completely with more pine needles. Keep children at a safe distance.

4. When all the needles have burned away, the mussels are ready (discard any that have remained shut). They are delicious eaten with crusty bread and butter, accompanied by a glass of white wine.

Black pudding and apple kebabs

Serves 6

60 cm (2 ft) length prime quality black pudding

2-3 green apples, depending on size

4 tablespoons lemon juice

1 tablespoon sugar

1 teaspoon ground cinnamon

salt, pepper

6 skewers

1. Light the barbecue 2 hours before the meal.

2. Cut the black pudding into 12 equal pieces.

3. Peel the apples and cut them into roughly 3 cm (1 inch) cubes, sprinkling on lemon juice to stop them going brown.

4. Make a mixture with the sugar, cinnamon and salt, drain the apple cubes and roll them in it.

5. Thread the black pudding on the skewers, with the apple pieces.

6. Grill the kebabs on the barbecue for 5 minutes each side, season lightly with pepper and serve quickly before they disintegrate.

TASTE BITE
ALL FORMS OF BLACK PUDDING (and also white pudding) can be prepared in this way.

Chicken kebabs with limes

Serves 6

6 chicken breasts, sliced part-way through and opened out

juice of 3 limes

1 tablespoon grated fresh ginger

1 tablespoon curry powder

1 teaspoon ras al-hanout

3 tablespoons olive oil

3 whole bird's-eye or very hot chillies (optional)

2 limes cut into 6 wedges

salt, pepper

6 skewers

1. Mix the lime juice, ginger, curry powder, ras al-hanout, oil and chillies (if using) on a deep plate.

2. Put the chicken pieces into this marinade, cover with clingfilm and let stand in the refrigerator for 3 hours, turning them from time to time.

3. Thread each chicken piece on a skewer between two lime wedges.

4. Cook on the griddle for 10 minutes each side. Season with salt and pepper if necessary.

TASTE BITE

RAS AL-HANOUT is an exotic and complex blend of numerous spices including cloves, cinnamon, nutmeg, cardamon, peppercorns, used in Moroccan and Tunisian cuisine.

Spiced beef kebabs

Serves 6

1 kg (2 lb) beef fillet, cut in large cubes

1 tablespoon ground ginger

1 pinch nutmeg

juice of 1 orange

juice of 1 lime

1 tablespoon thin, clear honey

salt, pepper

6 skewers

1. Mix the ginger, nutmeg, orange juice, lime juice and honey in a bowl. Season with salt and pepper.

2. Put the cubes of meat into this marinade and stir well to ensure they are thoroughly coated. Cover with clingfilm and set aside for 1 hour at room temperature.

3. Divide the meat between the skewers; lay them on the barbecue and cook for 5 minutes, turning often. Serve hot.

TASTE BITE

SERVE with chips and a mixed green salad.

Lamb kebabs Oriental style

Serves 6

750 g (1½ lb) lamb, cut into small cubes

1 tablespoon sunflower or groundnut oil

2 teaspoons ras al-hanout (see Taste Bite, page 64)

1 pinch cinnamon

1 pinch chilli powder

Sichuan (or Chinese) pepper

6 merguez (spicy North African sausages), or other spicy sausage, each cut into 4 pieces

salt, pepper

6 skewers

1. Put the oil with the spices on a deep plate.

2. Add the lamb and mix well to ensure the pieces are coated, then season with salt and pepper. Cover with clingfilm and leave in a cool place for 12 hours.

3. When the barbecue is ready, thread the lamb cubes onto skewers, alternating them with the merguez.

4. Place them on the grill and cook for 5 minutes on either side.

TASTE BITE

A TABOULEH, OR COUS-COUS flavoured with coriander and a handful of raisins, is the classic accompaniment to this dish.

Veal kebabs with oranges

Serves 6

1 kg (2 lb) veal fillet, cut in small cubes

1 bunch lemon thyme

2 juicy oranges with untreated skins

4 tablespoons lemon juice

1 teaspoon sugar

2 tablespoons olive oil

salt, pepper

6 skewers

1. Rub the leaves from the thyme.

2. With a potato peeler, remove the rind from the oranges in long, fine strips, then squeeze the juice.

3. Mix the orange and lemon juices, the thyme, sugar, oil and salt and pepper in a deep dish.

4. Add the cubes of veal and marinate for 6 hours in the refrigerator, turning them from time to time.

5. Light the barbecue well in advance so that the embers are very hot.

6. Thread the meat and the pieces of orange rind alternately on skewers and cook on the grill for 10 minutes on each side.

TASTE BITE

PINK OR YELLOW grape-fruit may be substituted for the oranges if preferred.

Magrets of duck kebabs with dried figs

Serves 6

3 magrets (breasts of dark-fleshed ducks)

6 dried figs

1 tablespoon Armagnac

salt, pepper

6 skewers

1. Soak the figs in the Armagnac, diluted with a little water.

2. Cut the magrets into pieces, season with salt and pepper and set aside.

3. When the figs are softened, drain them and dry on kitchen paper.

4. Thread them on the skewers, alternating with the pieces of duck.

5. Set the kebabs on the barbecue, skin side down, and grill for 3 minutes then turn them over and cook for a further 1–3 minutes, according to preference.

TASTE BITE
ACCOMPANY this dish with an unsweetened apple purée, seasoned with salt and pepper.

Turkey kebabs

Serves 6

1 kg (2 lb) turkey breast

2 tablespoons sunflower or groundnut oil

1 tablespoon Worcestershire Sauce

20 spring onions peeled and cut in half

¹/₂ teaspoon curry powder

36 cherry tomatoes

salt, pepper

6 skewers

1. Cut the turkey meat into about 2 cm (³/₄ inch) cubes.

2. Stir the oil, Worcestershire Sauce, spring onions, curry powder and the turkey meat together in a bowl. Season with salt and pepper and chill in the refrigerator for at least 2 hours.

3. Thread the cubes on skewers, alternating with the cherry tomatoes and spring onions.

4. Grill on the barbecue for 5 minutes, correct the seasoning if necessary and serve.

TASTE BITE

YOU COULD SERVE Spanish rice with these kebabs.

Wild boar kebabs

1 saddle of wild boar

3 shallots, halved

3 leaves fresh sage

3–4 stems fresh mint

2 bay leaves

3 sprigs thyme

¹/₂ bulb of garlic, cut horizontally

500 ml (¹/₂ bottle) good red wine

2 tablespoons groundnut oil

6 peppercorns

2 cloves

salt

6 skewers

1. Cut the meat in 3 cm (1 inch) cubes.

2. In a bowl, prepare a marinade with the rest of the ingredients.

3. Stir in the cubes of meat, cover with a cloth and leave in a cool, dark place for several hours.

4. Drain the meat and thread onto skewers. Grill them on the barbecue for 7–10 minutes on each side according to taste and the tenderness of the meat.

TASTE BITE

SERVE this dish with plain boiled potatoes and warm redcurrant jelly.

Quails stuffed with raisins

Serves 6

12 dressed quails

100 g (3¹/₂ oz) raisins

1 glass good quality rum

12 thin slices smoked bacon

12 bay leaves

100 g (3¹/₂ oz) clarified butter

salt, pepper

6 long skewers

1. Pour the rum over the raisins and leave to soak for 30 minutes.

2. Stuff the quail with the rum-soaked raisins then lay a bay leaf on the breast of each bird and wrap them in the slices of bacon.

3. Brush over the quails with clarified butter.

4. Thread the quails, 3 at a time, on long skewers and cook slowly for 15 minutes, turning constantly.

5. Let them rest on the edge of the barbecue for 10 minutes then season with pepper and a little salt and serve.

TASTE BITE

EAT THE QUAILS with potatoes sautéed in goose or duck fat.

vegetable
dishes

Garlic and shallots with olive oil

Serves 6

1 bulb garlic (new season, preferably)

6 red shallots

Aromatic Olive Oil (see page 10)

salt, pepper

6 skewers

1. Separate the garlic cloves and skin them. Also skin the shallots, cutting them into 2 or 3 pieces, according to size.

2. Thread the garlic and shallots onto thin wooden sticks and blanch them for 10 minutes in boiling water.

3. Drain the kebabs and dry on kitchen paper. Brush all over with Aromatic Olive Oil or oil of your choosing.

4. Lay them on the hot grill of the barbecue, at the highest position, and let them cook for 10 minutes on each side. Season with salt and pepper.

TASTE BITE
GARLIC AND SHALLOTS done in this way can be served with a grilled beef rib, or lamb cutlets.

Asparagus cooked on the griddle

Serves 6

**24 slender
asparagus spears**

olive oil

salt, pepper

1. If the asparagus spears are too thick, slice them in half lengthways.

2. Blanch the spears for 3 minutes in boiling salted water, then cool immediately in a bowl of iced water. Drain on kitchen paper.

3. Brush over the spears with olive oil and set aside until needed.

4. At the last moment, grill the spears for 1 minute each side on a very hot griddle.

5. Season with salt and pepper and serve.

TASTE BITE

THESE ARE A REAL TREAT served with wafer-thin slices of raw serrano ham (Spanish wild boar ham).

Grilled aubergines

Serves 6

3 large shiny, firm aubergines

2 tablespoons olive oil

sea salt, pepper

1. Brush the aubergines all over with olive oil.

2. Place on the barbecue to grill at medium heat for 5–10 minutes, then turn them over and grill for a further 10–15 minutes, brushing lightly with olive oil, if necessary.

3. Season with salt and pepper and serve immediately.

TASTE BITE

THIS DISH, together with some garlic purée, would be good served with lamb.

Mixed vegetable kebabs

Serves 6

3 courgettes

12 cherry tomatoes

2 yellow or red peppers

12 fresh pearl onions

3 tablespoons olive oil

1 bunch lemon thyme

rosemary twigs

salt, pepper

TASTE BITE
THE PEARL ONIONS could be replaced by spring onions, which would not need boiling.

1. Slice the courgettes in half lengthways, remove the seeds with an apple corer and cut the halves into about 3 cm (1 inch) lengths.

2. Blanch the courgette pieces for 3 minutes in boiling salted water then refresh in iced water and drain.

3. Blanch the cherry tomatoes in boiling water for 10 seconds then skin them.

4. Remove the stem and the seeds from the peppers and cut into pieces.

5. Peel the pearl onions and boil them for 5 minutes.

6. Pour the olive oil into a deep plate and add the leaves rubbed from the lemon thyme.

7. Dip all the vegetables in this oil then thread them on the rosemary twigs (or small wooden sticks). Season with salt and pepper and cook slowly on the grill of the barbecue, over hot embers, for 10 minutes.

8. Check the seasoning before serving.

Carrots with cumin seeds

Serves 6

3 large old season carrots

1 tablespoon softened clarified butter

1 tablespoon sugar

1 teaspoon cumin seeds

salt, pepper

6 skewers

1. Scrape the carrots and slice them lengthways into fine strips with a potato peeler. Blanch the strips for 1 minute in boiling salted water then cool immediately in iced water.

2. Drain the strips and dry on kitchen paper, then lightly brush over with the clarified butter.

3. Thread the carrot 'ribbons' along the skewers then dust them with the sugar, salt, pepper and cumin seeds.

4. Lay the ribbons on a hot griddle for a few minutes until they are caramelised. Serve immediately.

TASTE BITE

FENNEL SEEDS could be used instead of cumin and the carrots could be lightly dusted with ground cinnamon before serving.

Button mushrooms with bacon strips

Serves 6

24 medium button mushrooms

4 tablespoons lemon juice

100 g (3¹/₂ fl oz) melted butter

4 sprigs flat-leaved parsley, chopped

1 garlic clove, crushed

3 slices smoked streaky bacon, about 0.5 cm (¹/₄ inch) thick

salt, pepper

1. Trim the mushrooms, place in a dish and cover with the lemon juice to avoid discoloration.

2. Mix the parsley and garlic into the melted butter.

3. Cut the bacon into strips and blanch for 2 minutes in boiling water without salt. Drain, refresh in cold water and dry thoroughly with kitchen paper.

4. Wipe the mushrooms dry and thread them on skewers, alternating with the bacon strips.

5. Cook on the grill or griddle for 5 minutes, turning them frequently.

6. Add salt and pepper if needed and serve immediately.

TIP

IT IS IMPORTANT to choose very fresh mushrooms otherwise they may be rather spongy. Don't be afraid to cook them for a short time only; they are at their best when still crisp.

'Confit' potatoes

Serves 6

8-12 firm potatoes

**1 litre (1³/₄ pints)
duck fat or oil**

1 sprig thyme

1 bay leaf

**1 garlic clove,
lightly crushed**

salt, pepper

1. Peel the potatoes and cut them into thick rounds.

2. Put the duck fat into a sauté pan with the thyme, the bay leaf and the crushed garlic clove and place over moderate heat.

3. When the fat has turned transparent, add the potatoes and leave them to stew gently, at a constant temperature, for 45 minutes (the fat should barely simmer).

4. Lift the potatoes out with a perforated spoon and drain on kitchen paper.

5. Heat the barbecue then lay the potato slices on it, side by side, and grill for 2 minutes on each side. Season with salt and pepper and serve hot.

TIP

THE 'CONFIT' POTATOES can be prepared several hours in advance, placed on kitchen paper and kept at room temperature.

Fennel with dried apricots

Serves 6

3 good-sized fennel bulbs

4 tablespoons lemon juice

18 dried apricots

olive oil

1 teaspoon ground fennel

salt, pepper

6 skewers

1. Trim any damaged leaves from the fennel bulbs then cut them into slices about 1 cm ($\frac{1}{2}$ inch) thick (see illustration). Rub them with the lemon juice to avoid discoloration.

2. Soak the apricots in warm water for 15 minutes.

3. Drain the apricots and dry them and the fennel slices on kitchen paper, then thread them alternately on to pre-soaked wooden skewers. Brush them over with oil and season with salt and pepper.

4. Cook at low heat on the grill of the barbecue or on a griddle for 5–7 minutes on each side. Dust with the ground fennel and serve.

TIP

THIS BASIC RECIPE can be prepared with other dried fruits such as figs, prunes, small dried bananas, or anything else that takes your fancy.

Grilled corn on the cob

Serves 6

6 corn cobs

melted butter

salt, pepper

1. Strip off the husks from the corn, leaving just the tender inner leaves, and remove the silky threads.

2. Lay the cobs on the grill of the barbecue, over the embers, and cook slowly for 40–45 minutes.

3. When cooked, bring the cobs to the table with salt, pepper and the melted butter and eat with your fingers!

☼ TIP

YOU CAN SHORTEN THE COOKING TIME, and make certain the corn will be tender, by poaching the cobs for 10 minutes in a mixture of milk and water.

Grilled young artichokes

Serves 6

18 tender young artichokes

8 tablespoons lemon juice

1 tablespoon olive oil

Parmesan cheese

salt, pepper

 TIP

IF YOU ARE NOT CERTAIN THE ARTICHOKES WILL BE TENDER they may be blanched rapidly in boiling water before use. This could even be done the day before.

1. Trim the stems and the coarse outer leaves from the artichokes.

2. Cut them in half lengthways and rub with the lemon juice to avoid discoloration.

3. Brush over with olive oil and place them, cut side down, on the griddle. Cook for 4 minutes.

4. Season with salt and pepper and sprinkle with the Parmesan, either grated or flaked.

Grilled red peppers

Serves 6

6 red peppers

1 garlic clove, crushed

2 spring onions, chopped

1 teaspoon sugar

4 tablespoons lemon juice

1 bay leaf

1 teaspoon coriander seeds

salt, pepper

1. Char the peppers over the barbecue until the skins begin to blacken and then wrap them in newspaper and set them aside for 30 minutes.

2. Remove the skin and seeds, cut the flesh into strips and place in a bowl.

3. Mix the garlic, onions, sugar and lemon juice together and dress the pepper strips with this. Add the bay leaf and coriander seeds.

4. Check the seasoning and adjust if necessary before serving.

TIP

PEPPERS prepared in this way will keep for 48 hours in a cool place.

grilled
fruits

Grilled pineapple and mangoes

Serves 6

2 small pineapples

2 just ripe mangoes

sugar

salt with a touch of cayenne pepper

1. Cut the pineapples and mangoes into fairly large slices, about 0.5 cm ($\frac{1}{4}$ inch) thick.

2. Lay the slices of fruit on the griddle and grill until they are caramelised on both sides, then sprinkle with sugar and continue cooking for a few more seconds.

3. Lift the slices with a spatula and lay them on a long serving dish. Season with a touch of the salt mixed with cayenne pepper.

TIP

MELONS can also be pre-pared in this way.

Bananas with rum

Serves 6

**6 fairly firm
bananas**

**6 tablespoons
brown sugar**

rum

**3 vanilla pods, slit
in half lengthways**

1. Make a slit along the inner curve of each banana with a pointed knife.

2. Carefully prise the skin away from the fruit and insert 1 tablespoon of brown sugar, a few drops of rum and half a vanilla pod, then close and secure with string.

3. With the grill in the high position, place the bananas on the barbecue and cook slowly for 20 minutes. Serve warm.

TASTE BITE
THE MANDATORY ACCOM-
PANIMENT for these cooked bananas is vanilla ice cream.

Roasted figs with honey

Serves 6

18 fresh figs

1 tablespoon clarified butter

3 tablespoons thin, clear honey

1 pinch ground star anise

1. Brush the figs all over with clarified butter.

2. Place the figs on the barbecue grill, lifted to the highest level, or on a griddle at low heat. Cook for 10 minutes, turning frequently.

3. While they are cooking, mix the honey in a small bowl with the ground star anise.

4. When the figs are cooked, lift them gently from the barbecue and baste with the anise-flavoured honey.

TASTE BITE

EXCELLENT served with a good natural yogurt.

Roasted peaches with pistachio nuts

Serves 6

6 large, fragrant white peaches

2 tablespoons softened clarified butter

2 tablespoons coarsely chopped pistachio nuts

1 tablespoon brown sugar

1. Peel the peaches: if necessary, first make a slit in the skin and blanch them for 1 minute in boiling water, then cool in iced water.

2. Cut each peach in half and brush all over with clarified butter.

3. Place them on the barbecue, with the grill in the high position, or on a griddle. Leave to cook gently for 10 minutes, turning frequently.

4. Mix the pistachios and the sugar on a plate and roll the peaches in the coating before serving.

Cinnamon apples

Serves 6

6 cooking apples

6 teaspoons sugar

6 teaspoons butter

**1 tablespoon
ground cinnamon**

1. Core the apples with an apple corer
and place each one on a large sheet of
aluminium foil.

2. Put 1 teaspoon of sugar and
1 teaspoon of butter in the cavity of
each apple.

3. Sift the ground cinnamon over the
apples.

4. Wrap the apples completely in the
foil, place on the grill of the barbecue,
or on the griddle, and cook very slowly
for 30 minutes.

TASTE BITE
SERVE THE CINNAMON
APPLES with double cream,
or Greek yogurt.

by way
of accompaniment

Preserved lemon sauce

Serves 6

**2 lemons,
preserved in salt**

**50 pitted black
olives**

**1 bunch of
coriander**

**1 tablespoon thin,
clear honey**

**7 tablespoons
olive oil**

1. Halve the lemons then cut them into thin slices.

2. Cut the olives into slivers. Roughly chop the coriander.

3. Add these ingredients to the lemons and pour on the honey and the olive oil.

4. Mix well and taste – it's delicious and refreshing.

TIP

DON'T SKIMP ON THE HONEY, especially if you don't care for too much acid.

Coulis of yellow peppers

Serves 6

**6 large yellow
peppers**

1 teaspoon sugar

**2 tablespoons olive
oil**

salt, pepper

1. Thread the peppers on a long skewer and char over the flames of the barbecue until they brown – taking care not to burn your hands in the process.

2. Put the peppers into a colander to cool, then peel and deseed them and purée in a food processor, or rub through a sieve.

3. Season with salt and pepper, then add the sugar and olive oil.

TIP

THIS LIGHT SAUCE makes a tasty accompaniment for grilled fish.

Concassé of tomato

Serves 6

8 large, firm tomatoes

4 tablespoons lemon juice

1 tablespoon olive oil

1 garlic clove, finely chopped

8 sprigs basil, finely chopped

1 teaspoon sugar

1 teaspoon soy sauce

salt, pepper

1. Place the tomatoes in a bowl and pour over boiling water to cover. Leave for 1–2 minutes, then drain, cut a cross at the stem end of each tomato and peel. Remove the seeds and cut the flesh into small cubes.

2. In a salad bowl beat the lemon juice with the other ingredients of the dressing to form an emulsion. Stir in the tomato pulp carefully and cover with clingfilm.

3. Let stand in a cool place for 1 hour before using.

TASTE BITE

MINT, CHIVES OR CORIANDER may be used instead of basil. Balsamic vinegar may also be substituted for the lemon juice, but in that case the soy sauce should be omitted.

TIP

THIS LIGHT SAUCE makes an ideal accompaniment for grilled fish.

Tapenade

Serves 6

3 salted anchovies

150 g (5 oz) pitted black olives

1 tablespoon capers in vinegar

3 tablespoons olive oil

pepper

1. Rinse the anchovies under cold running water to wash off the salt.

2. Put all the ingredients into a food processor or liquidiser, or rub through a sieve, and reduce to a fine purée: that's all there is to it!

TASTE BITE

THIS RECIPE is also very good made with green olives.

TIP

THIS CLASSIC APPETISER from Provence also makes a delicious accompaniment for fish or meat, either on its own or spread on toast.

Pesto

Serves 8–10

5 new-season garlic cloves, peeled

1 bunch of basil

150 g (5 oz) grated Parmesan cheese

200 ml (7 fl oz) olive oil

salt, pepper

1. Pound the garlic in a mortar. Add the basil and continue to pound until smooth then add the Parmesan.

2. Keep on pounding while you drizzle in the oil in a fine stream. Season with salt and pepper.

TIP

THIS GREAT CLASSIC from Italy goes admirably with most fish and vegetables.

Sauce verte (green sauce)

Serves 8–10

1 bunch of flat-leaved parsley

1 bunch of chervil

8–12 tablespoons lemon juice

1 strip hot red pepper

1 garlic clove, chopped

4 tablespoons olive oil

1 tablespoon water

salt, pepper

1. Finely chop the parsley and chervil.

2. Beat all the dressing ingredients to form an emulsion and pour over the chopped parsley and chervil and mix.

3. Set aside for 1 hour before tasting it and adjust seasoning accordingly.

TIP
ALMOST ANY HERBS can be used in the preparation of this sauce.

Tartare Sauce

Serves 8–10

3 hard-boiled egg yolks

250 ml (8 fl oz) sunflower or groundnut oil

2 tablespoons lemon juice

1 spring onion, finely chopped

1 bunch of chives, chopped

200 g (7 oz) thick mayonnaise

salt, pepper

1. Mash the egg yolks to a smooth paste. Season with salt and pepper and keep mashing while drizzling in the oil.

2. Still mashing, add the lemon juice. Carefully mix in the spring onion, chopped chives and the mayonnaise. Correct the seasoning if necessary.

TIP
GRILLED MEATS, FISH AND VEGETABLES are all enhanced by the addition of this extremely simple sauce.

Barbecue sauce

Serves 8–10

6 tablespoons olive oil

3 onions, finely chopped

2 garlic cloves, crushed

1 green pepper, cut into very fine strips

200 g (7 oz) concentrated tomato purée

4 tablespoons thin, clear honey

1 glass red wine

500 ml (17 fl oz) chicken stock, made with a cube

1 tablespoon strong mustard

1 tablespoon sherry vinegar

6 tablespoons Worcestershire Sauce

1 bunch of basil

salt, pepper

1. Heat the olive oil in a sauté pan and soften the onions, garlic and green pepper.

2. When they begin to brown add the concentrated tomato purée, honey, wine and stock. Season with salt and pepper and leave to simmer over a low heat for 15 minutes.

3. Add the mustard, sherry vinegar and Worcestershire Sauce and cook for a further minute.

4. Chop the basil, and add at the last moment.

TASTE BITE
BARBECUE SAUCE traditionally accompanies grilled pork or beef.

Aïoli

Serves 6

**1 garlic clove,
crushed**

1 egg yolk

**1 tablespoon
strong mustard**

**250 ml (8 fl oz)
olive oil**

**2 tablespoons
lemon juice**

**1 pinch saffron
threads infused in
1 teaspoon hot
water**

salt, pepper

1. Pound the garlic in a mortar then incorporate the egg yolk, mustard, salt and pepper.

2. Drizzle in the oil, using an electric whisk, if possible, to whip the mixture, as if making mayonnaise.

3. When the aïoli is thick and firm, add the lemon juice and the saffron and make any necessary adjustment to the seasoning.

TASTE BITE
AÏOLI can be served with any kind of fish or vegetable

Tomato and fresh mint chutney

Serve 6

6 tomatoes

2 tablespoons olive oil

1 onion, finely chopped

1 tablespoon raisins

1 tablespoon sugar

1 green pepper, finely chopped (optional)

1 teaspoon mild curry powder

juice of 1 lime

fresh mint leaves

salt, pepper

1. Place the tomatoes in a bowl and pour over boiling water to cover. Leave for 1–2 minutes, then drain, cut a cross at the stem end of each tomato and peel. Remove the seeds and cut the flesh into small cubes.

2. Heat the olive oil in a sauté pan and soften the onion in it.

3. Add the diced tomato, raisins, sugar, green pepper, if using, and curry powder. Lightly season with salt and pepper and sprinkle on the lime juice. Reduce over a low heat for about 10 minutes, adding a little extra water if needed.

4. Strew with mint leaves just before serving.

TIP

THIS CHUTNEY is a little more original than the usual mango chutney and makes an excellent accompaniment to white meats and fish.

A barbecue is a simple device and fun to use: two large stones or a few bricks, some wood, a match and there you are – all ready to make a start! This open-air cooking equiment, originally a crude basic affair, has now developed into something very sophisticated. Different brands have flooded on to the market, offering enthusiasts an increasingly wide choice of easy-to-use and safe appliances, powered by various heat sources: wood, charcoal, gas or electricity. The griddle, for example, is a metal plaque heated by a looped gas-pipe. Gatherings around the barbecue are now truly festive occasions; the following few simple rules should guarantee that they go without a hitch:

Important safety precautions

• Institute an absolute ban on the use of petrol or alcohol for lighting the barbecue. There are efficient alternative fire-lighting products on the market which can be used in absolute safety.

• Never leave a barbecue unsupervised.

• Never attempt to move a lighted barbecue.

• In protecting the environment you are also protecting yourself: never use a barbecue near to dry grass, thickets or woods that the merest spark could set ablaze.

• Remove all inflammable products from the vicinity (petrol, alcohol, gas, newspapers or paper napkins, all of which could catch fire in an instant).

• Children are always fascinated by fire; never allow them to play near the barbecue or approach it unsupervised.

• Avoid wearing clothing made from synthetic fabrics, or long, floating sleeves which could catch fire in a flash.

• And all you ladies – and gentlemen – with long hair; tie up those tresses!

• Be sure to have a bucket of sand, blankets, brooms or a fire extinguisher ready, to put out any fire before it has a chance to spread.

• At the end of the day, pour water on the coals to ensure that the barbecue is completely extinguished. Check and check again that there are no cinders left smouldering.

Essential equipment

• Oven gloves for safe handling of kebabs, grills and other utensils.

• Bellows for reactivating the embers when they die down.

• A good supply of skewers and sticks, and long-handled spatulas.

• Perforated aluminium foil to cover the embers and prevent the flare-ups caused by grease and oil dripping onto them. This is particularly important when cooking marinated items.

• Different kinds of grill – double, basket etc. – to facilitate food handling.

The right way to go about it

• Light the barbecue well in advance. It is the embers, not the flames which cook the food. Length of time needed to prepare the barbecue before cooking can begin: 45 minutes for charcoal (the most popular among enthusiasts); at least one hour, even several hours, for wood, which is still the authentic fuel.

• Be sure to produce plenty of embers – the larger the items and the longer the cooking time, the more embers will be required. For a leg of lamb, for example, you will need to have enough wood or charcoal available to keep the fire going for at least 2 hours before cooking begins.

• Use tongs or bellows to speed up the rate at which the charcoal burns.

• Reduce the heat by raking ash over the embers. Some foods, like vegetables, need a lower heat.

• If you are using a modern barbecue, follow the manufacturer's instructions to the letter. Properly used, these appliances require much less preparation time.

marinades

small dishes and kebabs

Fish

large dishes

Meat

vegetable dishes

by way of accompaniment

grilled fruits

Acknowledgements:

Lorraine Barbier, Sophie Dehillerin, Sophie Boucot,
Martine Descamps, BVH, Habitat, The Conran Shop,
Compagnie Française de l'Orient et de la Chine,
Le Bon Marché.

**This book first published in France by EPA, a division of
Hachette-Livre**

**This edition first published 2003 by Hachette Illustrated UK,
Octopus Publishing Group, 2–4 Heron Quays, London E14 4JP**

Translation copyright Octopus Publishing Group

**English translation: Translate-A-Book, Oxford
Typesetting: Organ Graphic, Abingdon**

Editor
Brigitte Leblanc

Design
Nancy Dorking

Layout
Nadine Gautier-Quentin

Typesetting
Monique Brétillard

Proofreading
Chloé Chaveau

Platemaking
Eurésys, à Biasieux

Printing
Tien Wah Press

Registration of copyright
No. 1317 – June 2000

ISBN: 1842021885